Let's Discov

Se

# Vaisakhi

*Celebrations & Birth of the Khalsa*

*Paramjit Singh*

D.T.F Publishers & Distributors
117 Soho Road, Handsworth, Birmingham B21 9ST, UK
Tel. : (+44) 0121 515 1183/551 7898
Fax : (+44) 0121 554 2676
email : info@dtfbooks.com
website : www.dtfbooks.com



Cover & Book Design : H. S. Sev

Illustrations : Amarjeet Virdi

Author Paramjit Singh


First Published 2003

ISBN 1-901363-17-1

Price : £ 4.99
US $ 7.00

# *Let's Discover*

Vaisakhi is a publication which describes the celebration of Vaisakhi, both culturally and religiously. With beautiful illustrations, this book has been designed and written for children.

This book is part of a series of publications, written for the children. The series "Lets Discover" are DTF Books own publications, which have been commissioned to enlighten and educate children.

Key to the success of DTF Books is the values to strive for innovation and creativity in learning methods. In addition to increasing the awareness of the diversity of cultures and the enriching prospects for more cross cultural activities and resources.

We hope you will enjoy this book and look forward to our forthcoming publications

D.T.F Publishers & Distributors
U.K

**I**ndia the land of festivals, with many different religions and languages, celebrates many festivals throughout the year such as Holi, Dusshera, Diwali, Vaisakhi, with many more to name.

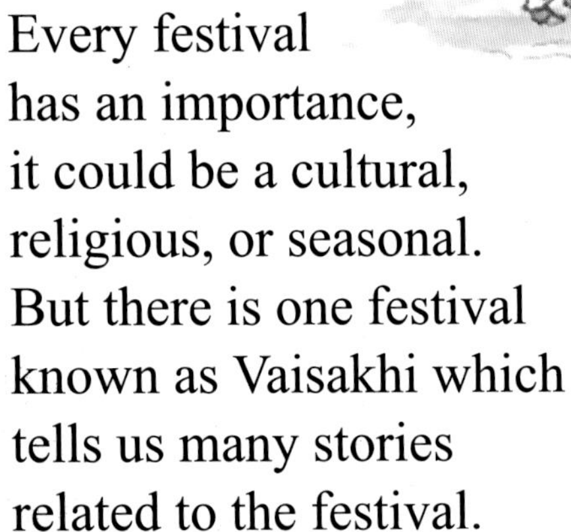

Every festival has an importance, it could be a cultural, religious, or seasonal. But there is one festival known as Vaisakhi which tells us many stories related to the festival.

Vaisakh is the first month of the Indian solar calendar which falls around the first day of the month of Vaisakh, ( the Vaisakhi day) that fell on March 30th in 1699 AD-now celebrated on April 13th.

The first day of the year, known as Vaisakhi is celebrated in Panjab, Haryana,Himachal Pardesh ( Northern Indian States ) and all over the world.

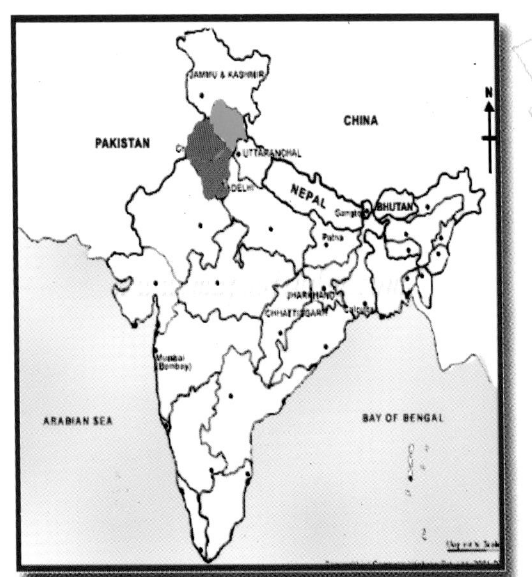


***For the Farmers of Panjab the crops are ready to harvest, and is a cause for celebration.***

***Every one looks forward to the new year ahead with hope of prosperity.***

***A day to mark the birth of the Khalsa.***

Vaisakhi holds a very special importance for the people of Panjab. Being an agricultural state they depend very much on the harvest.

A selection of fine oats, barley, wheat and other crops can be seen being collected and sold by the tones .

Supplies have to be sent and distributed throughout India.. The farmers look forward to the fine crops.

A cause for celebration, and thanks giving to the god.

With their offerings from the takings from the first crops harvested, by not forgetting him **"who"** feeds us all.

In Panjab (the land of Green Revolution) particularly and in the northern belt of India in general, farmers perform their own prayers by visiting the  Gurdwara's and  Temples to rejoice and celebrate the festivity with happiness and joy.

During this time they start to harvest their crops.The fields can be seen for miles, full of vibrant fragrance emerging from the crops, clear blue skies, birds singing melodious tunes, men folk preparing for work cheerfully, one could feel the happiness all around.

Panjabi's look forward to and  welcome the spring joyfully, this is the time when wheat turns golden brown,  the days becomes longer giving more daylight and  wintry cold nights are over.

Women are equally involved in their husband's success and bliss.

The men are busy in the fields starting work very early in the morning and women make sure to be of help where required.

Every one admires, looking at the green and golden brown fields, a natural beauty to consider, brings happiness to the hearts of thousands.

Farmers are all getting ready to harvest these ripe crops, all the harvesting machines and other equipment is being prepared to begin the process

The whole process takes many days, all the family joins in, from a child to the oldest every one want to do some thing. Work shall begin early in the morning, as the weather is getting warmer now.

**I**f you happen to be in a village in Panjab. Men and women could be seen dancing, the **Bhangra** Dance with the vibrant beat of the Dhol (Drum)

This strenuous dance tells the story of the agricultural process, from tilling the soil through harvesting.

As the Dhol changes beats, the dancing sequence progresses, dramatizing plowing, sowing, weeding, reaping, and finally celebrating in full swing.

***Bhangra*** *dance was born sometime between the 14th and 15th centuries and is now known to be the one of the oldest folk dance. Bhangra is the climax of the hard season of harvest when farmers celebrate by singing and dancing to Bhangra songs, and the beats thanking the heavens, for what rich crops they have reaped.*

Children dress in traditional clothes of yellow and saffron which are also known as the colours of spring. In joy of Vaisakhi the children sing and dance.

They fly kites and take part in many other competitions.

They are happy with the beginning of a new term and moving to a higher class in the schools

Dressed in their typical folk attire, women, celebrate the day with **Giddha**. ( Folk Dance of Panjab for women ) women and girls enjoy and dance, the vigorous Giddha performed by the Panjabi women wearing their traditional costumes and jewellery twirl and sway to the music.

***Giddha** This is a Panjab folk dance only performed by female dancers, Standing in a semi-circle, they clap and sing. Two of them advance away from the rest, sing and dance vigorously while others clap and join in singing, young ladies to express their inner feelings and emotions. Swaying in joyful mood, they communicate their thought through the melody.*

Presents and Gifts are exchanged amongst realitives, friends and the family. Every one looks forward to this event.

Different kinds of colourful mouth-watering sweets are distributed, such as Jalebees, Ladoos, Burfis and many more.

This is the time to look forward to the year ahead, so every one wants to be part of it. The elders, feel as they are at top of the world on this occasion.

They feel happy to see their families growing towards a better future.

Ladies prepare for the celebrations, buying new clothes for every one, as all wish to be seen in their best colourful outfits.

Cooking delicious food, an endless variety of Panjabi dishes are prepared, amongst these are favorite, Samosas, Pakoras, Halwa and many kinds of sweets etc.

Vaisakhi is celebrated with great enthusiasm. The preparations begin weeks in advance, as fairs along with many cultural events are established many days prior to the event.

Panjabi music is very popular, and during Vaisakhi, many folk singers perform, from folk music to the traditional Panjabi Bhangra Songs,

Famous singers of Punjabi folk music include
*Hans Raj Hans, Gurdass Mann, Yamla Jatt, Assa Singh Mastana, Mohinder Kapoor, Surinder Kaur, Parkash Kaur and others.*

Their songs describe the jubilation of Vaisakhi, along in a poetic form a detailed description of the beautiful young women of Panjab
and for a successful rewarding harvest

On the day of Vaisakhi. Sikhs all over the world visit local Gurdwara's (Sikh temples) and listen to keertan, (religious songs) Hymns, and discourses, and seek the guru's blessings for the future.

People offer fruits, soft drinks, sweets, which are distributed amongst the congregation, every one is in the festive mood and enjoy.

After the prayers, Karah Prasad (sweetened semolina) is served to the congregation, every one congratulate one another, the elders are happy blessings the young.

Processions
are taken out
which every one joins in,
from the youngest to the eldest
in their thousands.

At the head of which are the Panj Pyare (The five beloved ones )

Followed by in a purpose  made vehicle, is the Sri Guru Granth Sahib
( The  Holy Sikh Scriptures ) along with the head priests and singers.

A mini fair (Mela) can be seen outside the Gurdwara.
At the Mela shoppers set up small shops selling all kinds souvenirs, toys, artefacts. displaying the rich, glorious and traditional culture of Panjab.

While others prepare and cook many kinds of hot Pakora's, Samosa's, Jalebees, Ladoos, Gulab Jamuns…

The Dhol players are making sure people enjoy and keeping the scene alive with the wild beatings on the Dhol drum.

Different sports are also played amongst these are the Famous Kabaddi, wrestling, archery, horse riding etc,

For people living outside India football, Cricket and other games are very common amongst them.

Football, matches are also held on a national level.

**Kabaddi** is a team sport. Two teams compete with each other for higher scores by touching or capturing the players of the opponent team.

The two teams fight for higher scores, alternating defense and offense. The court is as large as that for dodge ball.

A member of the offensive team, enters the opponents court to touch opponents one by one with hands or feet and returns to his original position, thus scoring points. he must keep calling, "kabaddi, kabaddi" during the offense.

If the defensive team captures him and interrupts his call, he must leave the court, and the offense finishes. Defending players try to stop him by tackling and holding.
If this is successfully done, they win a point.

The traditional Sikh martial arts known as **Gatka,** which people visiting the Mela look forward to see and enjoy.

Young Sikhs display their martial arts skills with the utmost respect on the beating of the drum.

Different groups hold tournaments for this traditional martial arts, performed by young men and their teachers.

**Gatka**

(Gatka goes back to about 1200 years, In the past few centuries, Gatka has mainly been practised in India by the Nihang Singhs, Gatka is a martial art originating from Panjab (North West of India). it was practiced by the Sikhs, to defend themselves against the enemy.

The effectiveness of Gatka has been proved for centuries, not just by the Sikhs but also the earlier practitioners of this art, Gatka is a battle-tested, ancient martial art that survives today as part of the Sikh culture, began in fifteenth century India, in the Panjab region.

At  Anandpur Sahib Gurdwara, the atmosphere is some what very different.

As this is the birth place of the **Khalsa. (** The Pure One ) religious gatherings called 'DIWAN' are held here, where large gatherings of people are seen enjoying the hymns, which are sung  by famous singers.

On this occasion people travel from all corners of the world, many are Initiated ( Baptized ) on this day

**The Khalsa**

The word "Khalsa" means (the pure one), Khalsa's are Sikhs which have undergone the sacred Amrit Ceremony initiated by the 10th Sikh Guru, Guru Gobind Singh. The Khalsa order was initially created on Vaisakhi Day 1699, with Guru Gobind Singh initiating 5 Sikhs and then in turn asking the five Khalsa's to initiate him. The Khalsa initiation ceremony is undertaken as part of ones own personal spiritual evolution when the initiate is ready to fully live up to the high expectations of Guru Gobind Singh.

All Sikhs are expected to be Khalsa or be working towards that objective.

The ballot singers, the Dhadis, sings in a poetic form, the events from the  Sikh history.

People enjoy and listen to these with great interest.

**Langar** (*food from the common kitchen served free of cost irrespective of any discrimination of caste & religion*) is served to thousands through out the day.

Although the tradition of Langar was started by Guru Nanak, it was put into practice by the third Sikh Guru' Amar Das.

Every one is welcome to join, and is expected to sit amongst all.

Langar is prepared in the Kitchen, this event is busy, as food is made for all attending the Gurdwara.

At times, the celebrations of Vaisakhi are held in parks, due to thousands of people visiting, food is prepared and is taken to the parks, where it is served in the open, and inside big marques, people enjoy sitting in the sun, and again every one is welcome to join in.

Many people attending the Gurdwara bring offerings of different types, fruits, crisps, sweets, soft drinks, all is served between young children.

Big fairs are held on this day at many different places, such as Gurdwara's, Parks, Schools,  Many people visit these fairs all dressed up in bright colours and cultural outfits.

There is a spirit of joy and happiness, celebrations and many diffcrent activities fill the fairs.

The children are seen flocking around the toyshops, hawkers and the jugglers and the swings, merry-go-rounds are their special attractions.

The women surround the bangle-sellers and ornament shops, with eye catching colourful designs and styles of bangles.

All are in the festive and dancing mood. Girl and Boys hold competitions for the best dancing performance's. The whole atmosphere thrives and all want to join in .

The colourful outfits and the dancing movements showing the true colours and the rich culture of Panjab.

In another corner the youths are seen in their beautiful costumes performing the folk dances of the Panjab – Bhangra (of boys) and Giddha (of girls) at the beats of the Dhol, a day celebrated by all dancing together.

Vaisakhi holds another importance for the Sikhs. Guru Nanak (The founder and the first Guru of the Sikhs) was born on 15th April 1469 and who worked towards creating a casteless society.

Guru Nanak was also the first person to introduce equality for both men and women.

According to Guru Nanak no one is to be considered high or low simply on account of caste and religion.

It was on the day of Vaisakhi, Guru Gobind Singh (The tenth Guru of the Sikhs) gave final touches to the teachings of Guru Nanak by creating the **Khalsa.** ( The Pure Ones )

In order to give a realistic approach to the teachings of Guru Nanak, Guru Gobind Singh also dedicated his entire life & struggled from the young age of nine years to establish a casteless society.

He wanted to create a strong and united body of Brave, fearless, courageous, helpful people. The People who could fight against the enemies of society and humanity of the time.

The act of transforming the Sikhs into the Khalsa was a highly dramatic event. Which coincided with the Vaisakahi festival.

In the beginning of the year 1699 AD, Guru Gobind Singh sent out invitation to all the Sikhs, to attend a special gathering on the occasion of Vaisakhi at **Anandpur Sahib**. On the given day, a large number of Sikhs arrived at Anandpur Sahib from far corners of the country.

In order to accommodate the gathering, a large beautiful tent was set up in the open space near Fort **Kesgarh Sahib**. A raised platform was prepared and the carpets were spread around.

The huge gathering of over eighty thousand people were present.
People were anxiously waiting for the arrival of the Guru.

They were very keen to take a look at the Guru and listen to his orders.

At last the Guru arrived. His appearance was altogether changed.
His eyes were shining like the stars; his face was pure and he was holding a shining naked sword. He looked like a warrior ready to jump into the battlefield.

The Guru said in a firm voice, " My dear Sikhs my beloved sons, today my sword wants to taste blood."

The Guru demanded, who shall come today, in the honour and tradition of laying down his life for his faith.

There was a hushed silence all around.
Many of the present people grew pale with
fear on hearing such a strange demand.

There was no immediate response to the call.
For the second time the Guru repeated **"A life for your faith."**

When the Guru repeated the same demand on the third occasion, a
man named Daya Ram stood up with his folded hands and bowed
his head said, "My lord, my head is at your service."

The Guru asked Daya Ram to follow him into an enclosed area behind the platform.

Soon the people heard the sound of  the sword. They also heard something falling to the ground.

A stream of blood flowing out of the enclosure could be seen. It meant for the people that Guru had beheaded Daya Ram.

After few minutes the Guru came out with blood dripping from his sword.

Again he demanded for another head. By this time people were terrified, but still another man named Dharam Das came forward to offer his head.

He was also taken away to the same enclosure and the Guru repeated the same action.

On seeing this, people started to slip away. The assembly grew smaller as the people were caught with terror.

A few even went to Mata Gujri (mother of the Guru ) to put forward a complaint against the Guru for his actions.

The Guru appeared once again and repeated his call for the third head.
People were in shock. This time Mohkam Chand, offered his head.
The Guru took him into the enclosure and treated him in the same manner.

After some time the Guru again came out with more blood dripping from the sword and demanded for another head. Sahib Chand, stood up this time. He was also taken into the enclosure and the same action was repeated thereafter.

By the time the Guru appeared for the fifth time,
many people had left with fear, the crowd reduced to less then half.

When the Guru demanded the head for the fifth time,
Himmat Rai stood up with folded hands and offered his head.
He was also treated the same way, as was the case with the previous four.

By this time, the Guru had demanded five heads and had taken all of them to the enclosure.

The congregation started to think the obvious, which was, the Guru coming out and asking for more. But the Guru did not arrive out soon. He took longer this time inside the enclosure.

When he came out, his appearance was once again changed. He was wearing Saffron coloured robe and turban.

His sword was in its sheath. His face was calm and glowing with brightness.

Five persons dressed exactly the same as the Guru,
followed him to the main raised platform in front of the gathering.

The assembled people were startled and shocked to identify them as the same, who had offered them selves earlier and now they were all alive and standing with the guru.

The Guru declared the five Sikhs as the

**"PANJ PYARE"**

**i.e. Five the beloved ones.**

He further declared, "From today the Sikh's shall be called as
the 'KHALSA' (The pure one).

Then the Guru prepared **AMRIT** (sweet sugared water stirred with
a Khanda (a two edged dagger) while chanting Gurbani (Hymns) from
the Sikh Holy Scriptures.

First the five beloveds drank AMRIT from the same vessel and then
the Guru requested AMRIT to be given to himself.

The Guru declared that every Khalsa who shall take Amrit, **Singh** and **Kaur**
will be added to their names. A tribute to people who had been fighting
for their identity for over 200 years.

**Singh** meaning a lion for Men
**Kaur** meaning a Princess for Women

The Guru gave the gift of **Bana**, (the distinctive Sikh clothing and headwear.)

The Guru also blessed the Sikhs with a distinct appearance and uniform.
And because of the distinctive turban which Sikh men tie around their hair each day, they stand out in a crowd and easy to identify.

The turban, a fine muslin evolved as means of managing long hair which is left unshorn as a sign of respect for God-given form.
The turbans colours and its shape when tied are matters of personal preference.

He also offered five emblems of purity and courage.

These symbols, worn by all initiated Sikhs of both sexes, are popularly known today as the **Five K's:**

1. Kesh, unshorn hair;
2. Kangha, the wooden comb;
3. Karra, the iron (or steel) wristlet;
4. Kirpan, the dagger.
5. Kachera, the undergarment ( Shorts ).

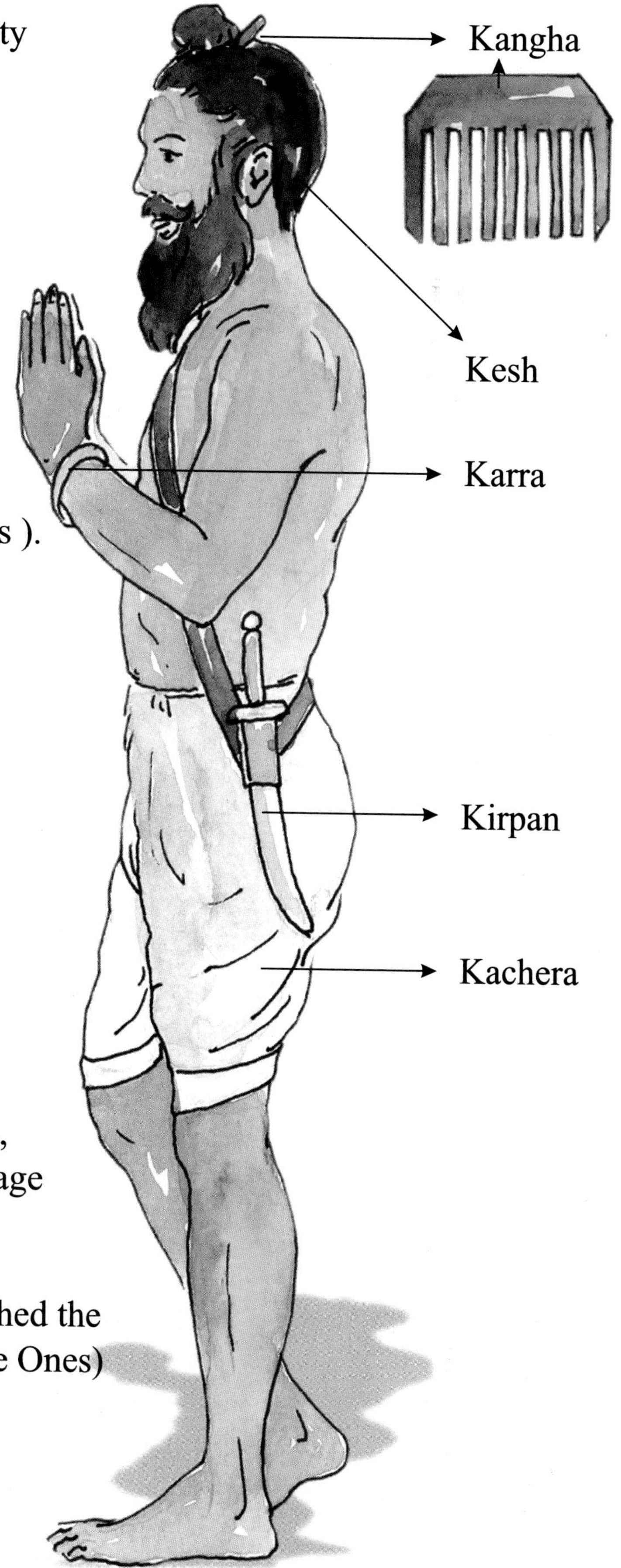


By being identifiable, no Sikh could ever hide behind cowardice again.

The Guru further said, "The Five beloved ones are in my form. They represent me. When ever and where ever five Amritdhari (initiated ) Sikhs come together, he **himself** would be present."

The Guru also said, "All those who receive Amrit from five beloved ones, will be infused with the spirit of courage and strength to sacrifice."

Thus with these principles he established the **Panth Khalsa**, ( the Order of the Pure Ones)

Giving the Khalsa a new and unique, indisputable, and distinct identity.

Thereafter the five beloved ones were renamed as:

Daya Singh
Dharam Singh
Mohkam Singh
Sahib Singh
Himmat Singh.

Thus, was born the 'Khalsa' on Vaisakhi of 1699 AD

***A Nation of Saint -Warriors.***

This is the meaning of the Vaisakhi of Guru Gobind Singh.

Because he knew at the time, an urgent need for a new fearless, courageous, protective, nation.

The Guru himself changed his name from **Gobind Rai** to **Gobind Singh**.

The Guru then invited others to take AMRIT, it is said nearly fifty thousand people were initiated in a matter of days.